Embracing

In the heart of winter, when daylight is brief,
The cold light awakens a bittersweet leaf.
Gentle hues glisten, a canvas so clear,
Inviting the wanderer, drawing them near.

Fires crackle warmly, stories unfold,
With laughter and memories, rich and bold.
As shadows grow long, and twilight draws near,
The chill of the night becomes ever so dear.

Spirits of the Frozen Pines

Whispers of pine trees, ancient and wise,
Echo through valleys beneath starlit skies.
Their guardian spirits, strong and serene,
Protect the secrets in spaces unseen.

Icicles shimmer, like jewels in the dark,
Mirroring dreams that ignite a warm spark.
As twilight descends on this mystical land,
Nature's pure magic, forever will stand.

Glittering Frost-Dripped Night

Under a sky of starry light,
Whispers of winter take their flight.
Each branch drips with crystal tears,
Silence wraps the world in fears.

Moonbeams dance on sheets of white,
Painting shadows, soft and bright.
Voices of the night arise,
Echoing through the frosty skies.

A chill that bites, yet feels so sweet,
The earth adorned in frost's retreat.
Footsteps crunch on paths untrod,
In this wonderland, we nod.

Time stands still in nature's grip,
As dreams of warmth begin to slip.
A glittering world where spirits roam,
In frosty silence, we find home.

The Palette of the Winter Wood

Beneath the branches, colors blend,
In icy hues, the seasons bend.
Scarlet berries, a touch of cheer,
Amidst the white, they persevere.

A tapestry of muted tones,
Rustling leaves, and creaking bones.
Soft whispers drift through trees so bare,
Reminders of warmth still linger there.

Sunlight filters through the frost,
Each ray reveals what we thought lost.
Nature's brush strokes here adore,
Crafting a landscape to explore.

Footprints trace a winding path,
Through woods that hold the winter's wrath.
Adventurers wrapped in layers tight,
Seek the beauty in pale twilight.

Celestial Auras in the Frost

Dancing lights adorn the night,
A symphony of soft delight.
With every breath, the magic flows,
In frosted air, the wonder glows.

Whispers of starlight paint the ground,
In silence deep, a world is found.
Each flake that falls, a cosmic kiss,
In sparkling darkness, there's no miss.

The sky weaves tales of frost-tinged dreams,
Where celestial color softly gleams.
A canvas vast, an artist's grace,
Embracing winter's cold embrace.

In shadows deep, the beauty hides,
As night unfolds, the magic bides.
Every twinkle, a tale untold,
In the winter's heart, we behold.

The Silent Guardians of Winter

Ancient trees in quiet stand,
Guardians fierce of this vast land.
With arms outstretched to cradle earth,
They witness all, from birth to dearth.

Snowflakes settle on mighty limbs,
In solemn silence, their hymn swims.
Protecting life beneath the snow,
A watchful eye where cold winds blow.

Time flows slow in this stillness fine,
With every breath, the world aligns.
Roots dig deep in frozen ground,
Holding secrets that abound.

Against the storms, they stand so proud,
Veiled in beauty, a winter shroud.
The silent guardians, ever wise,
In their embrace, quiet magic lies.

Winter's Lullaby in Green

Amidst the whispering pines,
Softly, the snow intertwines.
Nature whispers a tender song,
In winter's embrace, we belong.

Silent flakes fall from above,
Blanketing earth with a dove.
Evergreens cradle the night,
Holding the warmth, a soft light.

Gentle breezes cool the air,
Cloaked in white, without a care.
Each breath a cloud, pure and bright,
Winter's lullaby in the night.

Stars twinkle, a distant gleam,
In the stillness, we dream.
Cradled in soft, snowy ground,
Peaceful moments all around.

In this world, time stands still,
Nature's beauty, pure and shrill.
Whispers echo, softly sway,
Winter's lullaby, here to stay.

Veil of Frosty Splendor

A veil of frost paints the dawn,
On branches where sunlight's drawn.
Every twig adorned with care,
Whispers secrets in the air.

Icicles dangle, glistening bright,
Reflecting colors, pure delight.
Each step crunches, crisp and clear,
In this wonderland, we steer.

The world wrapped in a silver glow,
Where laughter dances soft and slow.
Breath becomes mist in the air,
Magic weaves warmth everywhere.

Frosted gardens, a sight so rare,
Beauty hidden, beyond compare.
Each petal wears a frosty crown,
Nature's art, never a frown.

Veil of frost, a transient grace,
Leaves a soft trace, a quiet space.
As daylight breaks, the chill will fade,
In splendor's glow, we find our shade.

Glistening Vows of the Trees

Through branches high, the sunlight gleams,
Whispers merge with gentle streams.
Frozen leaves, a sparkling sight,
Glistening vows, a heart's delight.

Each bough adorned with crystal lace,
Nature's promise, a tender embrace.
Rustling softly, a solemn cheer,
Dancing memories, ever near.

As seasons change with tender grace,
Time weaves stories, leaves a trace.
Through winter's chill, they stand so proud,
In their silence, they sing aloud.

The air is crisp, the world stands still,
With every breath, a quiet thrill.
Eternal oaths in the canopy,
In the heart of nature's symphony.

Beneath the sky, blue and vast,
Bound together, present and past.
Glistening vows whispered with ease,
Under the watchful, ancient trees.

Nightfall in the Evergreen Realm

As dusk unfolds its velvet shawl,
The evergreen whispers, beckons all.
Stars emerge in the dusky sky,
While shadows dance as night drifts by.

Moonlight spills on the forest floor,
A gentle glow, forevermore.
Each tree stands guard, a sentinel,
In nature's arms, we weave our spell.

Crickets serenade the cool air,
Nightfall brushes the world with care.
In this realm of evergreen dreams,
Peace envelops with soft moonbeams.

Whispers of winds through the leaves,
A chorus that every spirit weaves.
In the quiet, stories unfold,
Of ancient paths and secrets told.

As night deepens, we find our place,
Wrapped in nature's warm embrace.
In the evergreen realm of night,
Hearts awaken, feeling the light.

Nightfall's Whisper Beneath Pines

The dusk settles softly, shadows entwine,
Whispers of nightfall where stars softly shine.
Beneath ancient pines, the cool breezes sigh,
Crickets serenade as the daylight bids bye.

Moonlight cascades through the branches above,
A tapestry woven with threads of pure love.
Echoes of twilight, where dreams come alive,
Nature's sweet secrets in silence they thrive.

In the stillness of night, time seems to pause,
With each breath I take, the heart gently thaws.
The beauty of night wrapped in whispers so deep,
Beneath the tall pines, old stories we keep.

The Glisten of the Silent Woods

Amidst the tall trees where the stillness resides,
Sunlight trickles down, as the forest abides.
A glimmer of magic where shadows dance light,
In the heart of the woods, everything feels right.

Leaves gently rustle, secrets held tight,
Echoing moments that fade into night.
The glisten of nature, so vibrant and real,
Whispers of wonder in silence conceal.

With each step I take on the soft earthen bed,
I hear nature's hymn, the words left unsaid.
The glisten surrounds me, a world full of grace,
In the silent woods, I find my true place.

Arctic Embrace of Evergreen Dreams

In the land of the frost, where the cold winds roam,
Evergreen trees stand, a wintery home.
Whispers of snowflakes, a soft lullaby,
Wrapped in an embrace where the chill meets the sky.

Starlight reflects on the blankets of white,
Every breath, a moment, pure joy and delight.
The hush of the arctic, a serene, gentle gleam,
Lost in the wonder of evergreen dreams.

Frozen streams shimmer under moon's gentle gaze,
Nature's pure magic, in silvery haze.
In this arctic embrace, I find my true peace,
Among the tall pines, my heart finds release.

A Frosty Reverie

In the grip of the frost, the world fades away,
A frosty reverie starts with the day.
Mist dances lightly over meadows so wide,
Nature's soft canvas, where beauty won't hide.

Each breath forms a crystal in the chill of the air,
Whispers of winter, delicate and rare.
Snowflakes like diamonds, they twirl and they spin,
A dream woven softly where frost has been.

In the heart of the cold, warmth still can be found,
As the world paints its silence, a magical sound.
Through the frosty trees, my spirit takes flight,
In this serene wonder, I embrace the night.

Evergreen Embrace

In the forest's heart, so deep,
Where whispers of the ancients sleep,
Boughs embrace the gentle air,
A dance of life, so rich and rare.

Sunlight filters through the trees,
Kissing leaves with tender ease,
Nature's hymn, a soft refrain,
In every drop of falling rain.

Birds alight in verdant crowns,
Their songs resound, no hint of frowns,
A tapestry of green and gold,
The stories of the earth retold.

Underneath this timeless span,
Nature cradles every plan,
In the vast embrace of life,
We find solace, free from strife.

Evergreen, forever bright,
A haven in the fading light,
In this world, we find our space,
Within the evergreen embrace.

Crystal-Crowned Silence

In the stillness of the night,
Stars like diamonds, pure and bright,
A blanket of peace all around,
In this silence, magic is found.

Moonlight dances on the snow,
Softly whispers, gentle glow,
Every flake, a work of art,
A crystal crown set to impart.

Wind will tell tales of yore,
Of secrets held on winter's shore,
With every breath, the chill we take,
Revealing dreams that softly wake.

In this crystal-crowned embrace,
Time slows down in quiet grace,
Nature whispers in soft tones,
In the silence, we find homes.

Moments frozen, sharp yet sweet,
In stillness, every heart does beat,
A symphony of quiet night,
In this crystal-crowned light.

Shadows of Winter's Breath

The sun recedes, the shadows grow,
As winter wraps the earth in snow,
A breath of chill, a whispered sigh,
Beneath the pale and frosty sky.

Trees stand tall, their limbs adorned,
In silence deep, the night is born,
As shadows lengthen, softly cast,
The memories of autumn past.

In twilight's glow, the world stands still,
Nature rests upon the hill,
With every flake, a story spun,
In winter's breath, we are all one.

A hush descends, the stars alight,
Guiding wanderers through the night,
Shadows dance in soft embrace,
Life suspended, filled with grace.

So let the winter's breath unfold,
With warmth that lingers, stories told,
In the shadows, we find our path,
Embracing nature's quiet wrath.

A Shroud of White

Beneath the moon, the world sleeps tight,
A soft embrace, a shroud of white,
Each flake that falls, a whisper low,
Blanketing dreams in purest glow.

In the stillness, time stands clear,
Every heartbeat, every fear,
Wrapped in silence, cold yet sweet,
A shroud of white beneath our feet.

Footsteps echo, soft and light,
Tracing paths in winter's night,
A canvas fresh, untouched, and bold,
With stories waiting to be told.

Nature holds its breath in awe,
A tranquil moment, pure and raw,
In this shroud, we see the way,
For peace resides where shadows play.

As dawn breaks forth, let colors gleam,
In every heart, awaken dreams,
Beneath the white, the world will thrive,
In the shroud of white, we come alive.

Beneath the Frosty Veil

Whispers of winter softly call,
Silent night, embracing all.
Stars twinkle on a frosty sheet,
Nature's breath, peaceful and sweet.

Trees adorned in crystal lace,
Cold embraces every place.
Moonlight dances on the snow,
Beneath the veil, dreams softly flow.

Footprints fade with the morning sun,
Echoes of night slowly run.
Breath of winter, fleeting cold,
Stories of silence, softly told.

Beneath this shroud, all is still,
Yet the heart beats with a thrill.
In the hush, secrets reside,
Life awaits the spring's sweet tide.

So we wander, hand in hand,
Through this frosty, silver land.
Memories wrapped in winter's glow,
Beneath the veil, love will grow.

Glacial Hush of the Forest

A breath held tight in winter's breath,
Silent whispers, life and death.
Glacial mists weave through the trees,
Nature rests with tranquil ease.

Snowflakes tumble, soft and white,
Blanketing the world in light.
Branches arch with heavy loads,
While the forest gently dozed.

Footfalls muffled, dreams awake,
In this moment, hearts can quake.
Stillness reigns, a sacred space,
In the chill, find our embrace.

Ice crystals shimmer, spirits soar,
Echoes linger, forever more.
Among the trees, our shadows play,
In the hush, we dream away.

Awake the magic, feel the sway,
Nature's breath in soft ballet.
Together, we embrace the frost,
In this moment, love embossed.

Secrets in the Hoarfrost

Morning breaks with icy gleam,
Nature's canvas, pure and dream.
Hoarfrost clings to every branch,
Whispered secrets in a trance.

Patterns weave in pale embrace,
Time stands still, a sacred space.
In this chill, stories unfurl,
Frozen gems in a silver swirl.

Each breath hangs in the frosty air,
Life's heartbeat, tender and rare.
With every step, a tale unfolds,
In the still, the heart beholds.

Echoes of the night's retreat,
Sunrise, painting all complete.
In a hush that feels divine,
Secrets whispered, yours and mine.

Hoarfrost fades as day grows warm,
Yet in our souls, it keeps its charm.
Memories etched, forever cast,
In winter's grasp, a love steadfast.

A Ballet of Ice and Evergreen

Graceful limbs with frosty kiss,
Nature's dance brings pure bliss.
Evergreens in a silent sway,
Celebrate the winter's play.

Ice crystals shimmer, twirl and spin,
As the whispers of chill begin.
Each flake swirls in a perfect arc,
Touching hearts, igniting spark.

A symphony of cold and shade,
In this moment, magic made.
Snowflakes fall, like dancers bright,
In the hush of a starry night.

We twine amidst this frozen grace,
Finding warmth in winter's embrace.
Together, two hearts beat as one,
In the ballet until dreams are spun.

When the thaw brings life once more,
We'll remember this icy shore.
Dancing through the shadows sweet,
In the ballet, our worlds meet.

Enchanted Forest Dreams

In the heart of the wood, where whispers dwell,
Mysteries weave a magical spell.
Leaves rustle softly, secrets unsaid,
Guiding lost souls through paths that they tread.

Moonlight dances on shimmering streams,
Crickets serenade in soft, gentle dreams.
Each step reveals a story untold,
In this realm where wonders unfold.

Mossy carpets cushion my way,
As shadows linger and softly sway.
The scent of pine fills the air,
Inviting all who venture near.

With every glance, a new sight appears,
Echoes of laughter, whispers of fears.
In this haven, I find my release,
Boundless beauty, a feeling of peace.

Here in the forest, time stands still,
Nature's embrace, a gentle thrill.
Enchanted dreams take me high,
Beneath the vast and starry sky.

Frosted Fir Reverie

Under the weight of winter's sigh,
Frosted firs rise, reaching high.
Sparkling crystals dance in light,
Creating a world both pure and bright.

Snowflakes whisper as they fall,
Blanketing earth in a silvery sprawl.
Each branch heavy with nature's lace,
In this frozen elegance, I find my place.

Stillness surrounds, a hushed delight,
As stars twinkle in the deep, dark night.
The chill in the air, crisp and clear,
Fills my heart with warmth and cheer.

A soft crunch beneath my feet,
Echoes of solitude, calm and sweet.
In this frosted realm I roam,
Every breath feels like coming home.

Filled with wonder, the night unfolds,
Stories of winter in whispers told.
Wrapped in beauty, I softly sway,
In the frosted fir's embrace, I'll stay.

The Tranquil Boughs

Among the trees, where silence reigns,
Tranquil boughs offer gentle gains.
A soft breeze sows the seeds of peace,
In their shade, all troubles cease.

Sunlight filters through leaves so green,
Painting shadows, a picturesque scene.
Nature cradles weary hearts,
In her arms, a new journey starts.

Birdsongs echo, a lullaby sweet,
Each note a reminder to slow our beat.
With every rustle, they share their grace,
In the tranquil boughs, we find our place.

Time drifts softly, like petals in air,
Moments unfold without a care.
In this haven, life feels whole,
A sanctuary for the seeking soul.

With every breath, the world expands,
In sacred whispers, life understands.
The tranquil boughs, a gentle embrace,
Guide us to a brighter space.

Luminous Branches in Twilight

As twilight drapes its velvet shawl,
Luminous branches begin to call.
Glowing softly with day's last light,
Whispering secrets to the night.

Stars awaken, shy and bright,
Painting the sky, a wondrous sight.
Among the trees, shadows blend,
In this magical place, horizons extend.

Crickets chirp in rhythmic tune,
While the moon rises, a silver boon.
The air is filled with a tranquil hum,
As twilight beckons, and dreams succumb.

Each branch a canvas, stories displayed,
In ethereal hues that never fade.
Nature's gallery, alive and true,
In the soft glow of the evening dew.

Here in the twilight, magic aligns,
Where heartbeats echo with nature's designs.
Luminous branches hold the key,
To a world where souls can be free.

Awakenings in the Frosted Realm

In quiet mornings, whispers rise,
Frost-kissed grasses, soft and wise.
A world draped in shimmering white,
Awakening slowly to the light.

Trees adorned with crystal lace,
Nature's beauty in frozen grace.
Each breath a mist, so pure, so brisk,
Embracing stillness, a calming risk.

Beneath the frost, life stirs anew,
Promises hidden, dreams breaking through.
In this realm where silence reigns,
Awakenings dance through icy veins.

Soft rays filter through branches bare,
Encasing shadows in splintered air.
A melody flows from the ground,
In this frosted realm, peace is found.

Guardians of the Frozen Light

Silent sentinels, frozen tall,
Guardians of winter, standing small.
Their branches reach for skies so clear,
Embracing the chill, year after year.

A shimmer of ice, a cloak of white,
Holding secrets in the pale moonlight.
They whisper stories of ancient nights,
Echoes of magic in frosted sights.

Together they form a tranquil choir,
With every breeze, they never tire.
In twilight's embrace, they softly glow,
Guarding the dreams that linger below.

Their watchful gaze, a calming sign,
In the heart of winter, they intertwine.
A tapestry woven with silver thread,
Guardians of light where shadows tread.

Luminescence in the Stillness

In the hush of night, stars ignite,
Luminescent dreams take flight.
Snowflakes shimmer like lost pearls,
Whirling softly in winter swirls.

Blankets of white on slumbering ground,
Silence wraps the world, profound.
Gentle glimmers trace the earth,
Crystalline beauty, a moment's worth.

A glow beneath the moon's embrace,
Whispers of light in a tranquil space.
Stillness whispers secrets untold,
In the luminescence, hearts unfold.

Each breath a spark in the chilled air,
Reflecting wonder, a quiet dare.
In this stillness, magic blooms,
Illuminating the darkened rooms.

A Symphony of Icy Whispers

Beneath the sky, a symphony plays,
Icy whispers weave through the haze.
Each note a caress, crisp and bright,
Echoing softly on snowy night.

A harmony found in the stillness deep,
Painted in frost where shadows sleep.
Fingers of wind strum the trees,
Creating a song carried by the breeze.

Melodies rise from the frozen creek,
Carried with grace, tender and meek.
An orchestra swells in the snowy embrace,
Nature's concert, a timeless grace.

Harmonies clash, then entwine,
In a dance of snowflakes, pure and divine.
Listen close to the chilling sound,
As a symphony of whispers surrounds.

Frosty Whispers of the Woods

In the hush of morning light,
Frosty whispers dance with glee,
Branches draped in silver white,
Nature's soft tranquility.

Footprints pause on crunchy ground,
Echoes of the night retreat,
Gentle breezes whisper sound,
Winter's breath a soft heartbeat.

Pine trees loom like silent guards,
Veils of frost on every limb,
Nature's canvas, cold and hard,
Shimmers bright, a wintry hymn.

Buds of life lie deep and still,
Wrapped in dreams of warmer days,
Time's embrace, a gentle chill,
In this whitewashed, peaceful haze.

The world stands still beneath the sky,
In the woods, where secrets grow,
Frosty whispers softly sigh,
In the heart of winter's glow.

Ethereal Tapestry of White

A tapestry of purest white,
Covers earth in soft embrace,
Glimmers shine in morning light,
Nature dons her frosty lace.

Shadows stretch and softly blend,
Underneath the bending boughs,
Every flake a story penned,
On the ground, a silent vow.

Winter's breath sets hearts aglow,
Painting scenes of quiet peace,
In the chilly winds that blow,
Laughter echoes, joys increase.

Little critters scurry quick,
Through the drifts, their paths are drawn,
Each a wisp, a playful trick,
Chasing dreams 'til break of dawn.

The canvas of the world stands still,
In the realms of icy grace,
Ethereal, a winter thrill,
Nature's art in every space.

The Silent Embrace of Winter

Snowflakes fall, a soft caress,
Whispers linger, still and light,
In their dance, the world's duress,
Fades away in shades of white.

Every branch adorned in grace,
Huddled hearts find warmth within,
Winter's cloak, a soft embrace,
Time's rhythm slows, silence wins.

Streams are frozen, held in dream,
Underneath the icy sheen,
Nature's breath, a quiet theme,
A tapestry of serene.

Even stars in skies so clear,
Shimmer softly, whisper dreams,
Winter wraps us, holds us near,
In its arms, each moment gleams.

The world transformed, so pure, so bright,
In this silent, crisp retreat,
Winter's magic feels just right,
In the stillness, life's heartbeat.

Frost Adorns the Sentinels

Frost adorns the ancient trees,
Sentinels of time and tale,
Guardians of whispered breeze,
In their shadow, dreams unveil.

Icicles hang like crystal swords,
Glistening in the dusky light,
Nature writes her own accords,
Crafting beauty from the night.

Footsteps crunch on frozen ground,
Echoes of the past remain,
In the stillness, wisdom found,
Every flake a brief refrain.

As dawn breaks with hues of gold,
Radiance warms the icy morn,
Stories of the brave and bold,
In the frost, new dreams are born.

Frosty breath adorns each limb,
Winter's brush, a work of art,
In this world, so vast and dim,
Silence sings to every heart.

Twilight Idylls in the Frost

In twilight's grasp, the world turns light,
A whispering chill embraces the night.
Stars flicker softly, a guiding glow,
While frost-kissed dreams begin to flow.

Branches weave tales of silver lace,
Carried on breezes with delicate grace.
Each breath of winter, crisp and clear,
Fills the heart with warmth, drawing near.

The fading sun bows, a regal farewell,
As shadows stretch long, casting their spell.
The hush of dusk blankets the land,
Nature's pure beauty, a wonder so grand.

Footprints in snow mark journeys begun,
Towards flickering fires, away from the sun.
In pockets of stillness, the night unfolds,
Secrets of frost time gently holds.

Such fleeting moments, like stars in the sky,
Embrace them close, let worries fly.
In twilight's embrace, a hush resides,
A dance of the heart, where magic abides.

Shadows of Frost on Leaves

Under the canopy, shadows play,
Frost on leaves in the dawn's soft gray.
Whispers of winter crinkle and call,
A delicate veil over nature's sprawl.

In the stillness, magic fills the air,
Each frozen drop shows beauty rare.
Wandering paths seem to sparkle bright,
In shadows of frost, the world ignites.

With every crunch beneath the feet,
The heartbeat of winter, rhythmic and sweet.
Branches glisten like diamonds set high,
In the soft embrace of a pale blue sky.

Silent wonders, nature's design,
Every fluttering leaf tells a line.
So let us linger in this serene bliss,
In shadows of frost, find warmth in the kiss.

Days may grow short as the nights expand,
Yet beauty persists, a gentle hand.
In winter's eyes, a story we weave,
In echoes of frost, we learn to believe.

Winter's Jewel Among the Boughs

Among the boughs, a jewel so rare,
Glistens like magic, elegant and fair.
Each flake of snow, a soft embrace,
In winter's kingdom, we find our place.

Branches bow low, heavy with grace,
Nature's artistry woven in space.
With every gust, whispers come alive,
In winter's jewel, the heart does thrive.

The silence lingers, thick and deep,
A blanket of time where memories sleep.
Moments of wonder, tender and bright,
Captured in shadows, kissed by light.

The world adorned in a crystal crown,
Every step forward, a soft, gentle sound.
In the arms of winter, we find our peace,
Winter's jewel grants our hearts release.

Through the chill, there lies a warmth,
In every sparkle, a newfound swarth.
Let us cherish, as the seasons flow,
The beauty we find in winter's glow.

The Sigh of the Cold Woods

In the cold woods, a sigh takes flight,
Carried through silence, embracing the night.
Trees stand sentry, ancient and wise,
Beneath a blanket of twinkling skies.

Frosted whispers float on the breeze,
Nature's breath stirs with gentle ease.
Every branch and leaf, a story untold,
In the sigh of the woods, hearts unfold.

Moonlight dances on the icy ground,
Echoes of creatures, a soothing sound.
Shadows stretch long, casting their spell,
In the cold woods, we find where we dwell.

Every crackle beneath our feet,
Guides us deeper, a path so sweet.
In the shivering trees, peace draws near,
In the sigh of the woods, we conquer fear.

Nature's embrace, a balm for the soul,
Reminds us gently that we are whole.
In the chill of the night, let us roam free,
Finding solace together, you and me.

Whispers in the Frost

Whispers dance through icy air,
Secrets held with tender care.
Glistening in the morning light,
Nature's breath, a soft delight.

Footsteps muffled on the ground,
Silent echoes all around.
Trees adorned with silver lace,
A serene and frozen space.

Frosted branches gently sway,
As the dawn embraces day.
Each crystal spark, a fleeting glance,
In this still and quiet dance.

Rivers wrapped in glacial sleep,
While the world begins to weep.
Winter's chill, a tender muse,
Painting skies in frosty hues.

In this realm of cold and grace,
Beauty lingers in this place.
Whispers soft as winter's breath,
Eternally, we dance with death.

Echoes of the Winter Forest

Echoes linger in the trees,
Carried softly by the breeze.
Snowflakes fall like whispered dreams,
Nature's art in silver streams.

Branches laden with white blooms,
Silent shadows cast in glooms.
The forest breathes a gentle sigh,
As winter's song begins to fly.

Footprints trace the path of light,
A journey made through day and night.
Each step echoes through the wood,
In moments still, where silence stood.

Frozen ponds reflect the sky,
Where whispers of the past comply.
Stars awaken in the frost,
In dreams of warmth, not lost.

In every nook where echoes dwell,
Nature casts her timeless spell.
The winter forest, fierce yet kind,
A haven for the wandering mind.

Glimmers on Needle's Edge

Glimmers spark on needle's edge,
Tiny gems in nature's pledge.
Morning sun on frosty pines,
A twinkling dance, a world divine.

Each needle bearing nature's tears,
Whispering tales through the years.
Glistening like stars at dawn,
In the silence, dreams are drawn.

Walking softly through the haze,
Captured in the winter's gaze.
Every breath of cold and clear,
Invites the warmth of those held dear.

Rustling leaves, a fleeting sound,
In this sanctuary profound.
Glimmers fading, life moves on,
Yet in our hearts, they carry on.

With every step, a story we weave,
In the forest, we believe.
Glimmers on the needle's spine,
Forever etched, a love divine.

Frosted Dreams in Evergreen

Frosted dreams in evergreen,
Whisper secrets yet unseen.
In the twilight, shadows play,
Hiding hopes as night meets day.

Every branch holds memories tight,
Wrapped in whispers, veiled in light.
Softly glows the winter's gleam,
In this world of frozen dream.

Underneath the starlit night,
Nature shares her purest flight.
Each snowflake, a kiss from the past,
In dreams of evergreen, we last.

A chorus sings of years gone by,
As the moon ascends the sky.
Frosted air, a gentle tone,
In this moment, we are home.

Where the heart finds peace and rest,
Amidst the trees, we are blessed.
Frosted dreams, forever hold,
Stories wrapped in winter's gold.

Glistening in the Silent Dawn

A whisper breaks the still of night,
Soft hues spread with golden light.
The world awakens, calm and bright,
In every heart, a spark ignites.

Dewdrops dance on blades of grass,
Nature's jewel, a fleeting pass.
Each moment held, a breath to grasp,
As shadows fade, our hopes amass.

Birds take flight on newfound wings,
A symphony of life begins.
Underneath the sky's soft spins,
The silent dawn, where joy springs.

With every pulse, the world renews,
In vibrant hues, the morning brews.
A tender touch in violet views,
Where dreams awaken, bright and true.

Glistening smiles, the day's embrace,
In nature's arms, we find our place.
Each moment cherished, a slow pace,
In silent dawn, we leave no trace.

Echoing Steps in White Shadows

In winter's grasp, the silence speaks,
White shadows dance on icy peaks.
Footprints mark where courage seeks,
Echoes resonate, as daylight leaks.

Through frosted trees, the whispers flow,
Secrets buried deep below.
In every flake, a tale to show,
The pulse of life, in ebb and glow.

Chilled air bites with a sharp embrace,
A tranquil pause in time and space.
With every step, we find our place,
Amidst the stillness, a gentle grace.

Voices call from shadows cast,
Reminders of a long-lost past.
In winter's hold, we stand steadfast,
Each echo is a heartbeats' blast.

As night descends, stars gently gleam,
In peaceful dreams, we dare to dream.
In white shadows, life's a stream,
With echoing steps, a silent theme.

Shards of Light in the Cold

Fractured beams on frozen ground,
In crystal air, a silence found.
Each shard of light, a story bound,
A flicker bright, where hope is crowned.

Underneath the pale expanse,
Winter winds in quiet dance.
With every glimmer, a fleeting chance,
To pause and feel the world's romance.

Icicles hang like tales untold,
Nature's art, both sharp and bold.
In every glint, a warmth to hold,
A universe in stillness unfolds.

With breaths of mist in the crystal chill,
We seek the light, we seek the thrill.
In every shadow, a longing will,
To capture moments, to fulfill.

Shards of light in the cold of night,
A tapestry of dark and bright.
Together woven, a pure delight,
In winter's breath, we find our sight.

The Cradle of Winter's Hold

Deep in the fold of frosty air,
Nature rests, a lull in prayer.
Veiled in white, without a care,
The world awaits, a beauty rare.

Crystalline dreams on soft snow's bed,
Winter whispers, softly spread.
In quiet moments, fears are shed,
The cradle rocks where hope is fed.

Fires burn bright in homes we keep,
With stories shared, our hearts leap.
Through blustery nights, in peace we sleep,
In winter's embrace, the magic's deep.

Time seems to pause, a gentle sigh,
Beneath the vast and starry sky.
In the cradle of night, we fly,
To dreams unbound, where wishes lie.

From winter's hold, we find our way,
With every dawn, a brand new day.
In the cradle's warmth, we long to stay,
As seasons change, they softly sway.

Reflections in a Winter's Embrace

The snowflakes dance in silent grace,
Mirroring the still, white space.
Beneath the boughs of frosted pine,
Nature holds secrets, pure and divine.

In twilight's hush, the shadows grow,
Whispers of winds, soft and low.
Footprints left in glistening trails,
Tell tales of journeys, where silence hails.

The river flows, a frozen stream,
Reflecting starlight, a dreamer's dream.
Each shimmered flake, a moment caught,
In winter's grasp, all worries fought.

The world lies wrapped in a crystal sheet,
Where warmth and chill, harmoniously meet.
In winter's embrace, we ponder and feel,
The beauty of moments, tender and real.

So let us pause in this tranquil place,
And find ourselves in winter's embrace.
For every breath in the chilly air,
Is a reminder of the love we share.

Melodies of the Frozen Night

Underneath the crescent moon,
The world sings a forgotten tune.
Frosted branches softly sway,
As whispers of night lead the way.

In the quiet, the stars align,
Painting the skies with threads divine.
Each twinkle a note, each shadow a word,
In melodies sung, yet never heard.

The crispness lingers, a breath of chill,
Nature's song holds a magic thrill.
The wind, it weaves through barren trees,
Carrying secrets of winter's breeze.

As snowflakes fall, they softly play,
Creating harmony in a gentle ballet.
Each flake unique, each sound profound,
In the frozen night, beauty is found.

So listen close, as night unfolds,
The melodies of winter, timeless and bold.
In every silence, in every sigh,
Resounds the magic of the night sky.

Nature's Crystal Symphony

With every breath, the chill unfolds,
A symphony that nature holds.
Icicles hang like notes in tune,
Reflecting light from the pale moon.

The forests draped in shimmering lace,
Enchanting every weary face.
Streams whisper secrets, soft and low,
As winter's tune begins to grow.

Each footprint pressed on powdered snow,
Is music created, a rhythm to flow.
The wind composes, a gentle breeze,
Strumming the branches, a song to please.

In the stillness, the heart beats fast,
Capturing moments meant to last.
The crystal notes fill the air,
In nature's concert, beyond compare.

Join in the chorus, hear it play,
Nature's symphony, night to day.
Let every flake and ray of light,
Guide us through the frozen night.

Beneath the Icy Embrace

Beneath the coat of winter's chill,
Lies a warmth that time can't kill.
The ground sleeps deep, hushed and tight,
Awaiting spring's return to light.

Overhead, the clouds drift slow,
Holding secrets of ice and snow.
Branches wear their frosty crowns,
Creating silence in sleepy towns.

The world transformed in white and gray,
A quiet pause, a still ballet.
Underneath the icy skies,
Nature dreams as time just flies.

Every corner, every street,
Covered softly, a pillowed sheet.
In winter's grace, we find our peace,
And let our busy thoughts release.

So gather close, embrace the cold,
For in this stillness, life unfolds.
Each frosty breath, a moment shared,
In winter's arms, we are prepared.

Secret of the Frosted Glade

In shadows deep, where whispers breathe,
The frost weaves tales upon the leaves.
A secret kept in winter's hold,
A glade of wonders, pure and bold.

With every flake that drifts and falls,
The echoes fade within the walls.
The stillness wraps the world in white,
A magic spark, a quiet light.

Footprints show where only few
Have walked the path of silence true.
A hidden realm where dreams take flight,
In frosted glade, away from sight.

The trees stand tall, adorned in grace,
A frozen time, a perfect place.
Where nature hums a hushed refrain,
And winter sings its softest strain.

Each breath of cold, a tune divine,
The glade unfolds, a world benign.
Secrets dance in every breeze,
In frost-kissed sighs, we find our peace.

Winter's Gentle Caress

A tender touch of frosty air,
The world is wrapped in gentle care.
Each snowflake falls like whispered song,
In winter's arms, we all belong.

The landscape shimmers, pure delight,
Beneath the soft, enchanting light.
With every flurry, dreams ignite,
In winter's heart, the world is bright.

The silence speaks in shades of white,
A canvas vast, a breathtaking sight.
While shadows weave their tales of yore,
In winter's grasp, we yearn for more.

As twilight falls, the stars emerge,
In winter's song, our spirits surge.
A gentle caress from skies above,
In every flake, we feel the love.

To wander through this wonderland,
With open hearts, we take a stand.
For winter's grace, a fleeting kiss,
In every moment, find your bliss.

Echoes of a Frozen Night

In stillness deep, the night unfolds,
With echoes soft, the darkness holds.
A world of white, where shadows play,
In frozen hours, we drift away.

The moonlight glows on icy streams,
Reflecting all our silent dreams.
Each breath released, a cloud of mist,
In winter's hush, we find our tryst.

The stars shine bright on velvet skies,
Whispering tales of lullabies.
As frost adorns each branch and leaf,
In stillness found, we seek relief.

The night is young, the world asleep,
In frozen moments, secrets keep.
With every sigh, the echoes rise,
As winter weaves her lullabies.

In dreams we soar, where shadows glide,
In frozen nights, our hearts abide.
With every star, we find our way,
In winter's grasp, forever stay.

Beneath the Frozen Canopy

Upon the ground, a carpet white,
Beneath the trees, a world of light.
The branches arch, a frosted dome,
In nature's arms, we find our home.

The crunch of snow beneath our feet,
An echo sweet, a rhythmic beat.
Each step we take, in whispers heard,
Amongst the pines, the quiet stirred.

The air is crisp, the twilight glows,
In every breath, the winter flows.
A tapestry of white and gray,
In frozen hues, we lose our way.

The canopy, a shimmering sight,
Embracing all with gentle light.
Where time stands still in nature's grace,
And peace, like snow, takes its place.

With dreams that dance on frosted air,
Beneath the canopy, we share.
A world reborn in winter's glow,
Together forged in falling snow.

A Dance of Frosted Boughs

In winter's grasp, the boughs do sway,
With frosted lace, they dance and play.
Each crystal flake, a whispered sound,
In chilling breeze, their beauty found.

Beneath the moon, so bright and clear,
The shadows loom, the night draws near.
A gentle touch on branches bare,
In silence deep, they seem to care.

The stars above, they twinkle bright,
As frosted boughs embrace the night.
A waltz of shadows, soft and slow,
In nature's realm, where wild winds blow.

The cold air bites, yet hearts grow warm,
In winter's song, we find our charm.
A symphony of frost and light,
In every drift, the world feels right.

So let us witness, hand in hand,
This dance of frost in winterland.
With every breath, a new delight,
As boughs do sway, through day and night.

Nightfall on the Pine Range

The sun dips low, in hues of gold,
While whispers of the stars unfold.
The pines stand tall, in shadows deep,
A tranquil hush, where secrets keep.

As night descends, the world grows still,
With gentle grace, the moon will fill.
The pine range sighs, a soft embrace,
In twilight's arms, a sacred space.

The scent of earth and whispers near,
As owls awake, we pause to hear.
The rustling leaves, a quiet tune,
Under the gaze of silver moon.

With every breath, the night takes hold,
Embracing dreams, both shy and bold.
The pine range sleeps, yet hearts awake,
In nightfall's peace, the world we make.

A symphony of stars ignite,
As shadows dance in soft twilight.
The whispers of the night remain,
To guide our souls through pine and grain.

Silent Guardians of the Chill

Amidst the snow, the trees arise,
With outstretched arms against the skies.
Silent guardians, timeless and grand,
They watch o'er every drifted land.

In winter's chill, they hold their ground,
With sturdy roots, deep and profound.
Enshrined in frost, their whispers flow,
In stillness, ancient tales they show.

Boughs draped in white, a regal sight,
They stand with pride, defying night.
With every gust, a tale unfolds,
Of seasons past, of memories bold.

The silence sings of ages long,
Their strength and grace, a silent song.
Each flake that falls, like whispered prayer,
In unity with the frozen air.

For in this chill, we find our kin,
Embraced by trees, where dreams begin.
The silent guardians of the chill,
Stand watchful still, with steadfast will.

Glacial Breath of the Timberland

In the timberland, where shadows play,
The glacial breath weaves night and day.
A whispering fog drapes the ground,
In cool embrace, where peace is found.

The ancient trees, they stand with pride,
Their roots entwined in nature's tide.
A breath of ice through branches flow,
As time stands still, so pure, so slow.

The glistening snow, like diamonds bright,
Illuminates the winter night.
In chill and calm, the world holds tight,
To dreams that bloom in silver light.

In frozen grace, we walk so light,
With hearts aflame against the night.
The timberland holds secrets dear,
In every breath, the world feels near.

Through frosted paths, we wend our way,
In quiet moments, let spirits play.
The glacial breath sings soft and clear,
In nature's arms, we cast out fear.

The Frosty Tapestry Unfolds

Beneath the starry sky, so wide,
A world adorned in white, we glide.
Each branch, a shimmering lace,
Holds whispers of winter's embrace.

As twilight casts a gentle hue,
The night unveils a silent view.
In shadows deep, the snowflakes dance,
In this frosty realm, we take our chance.

The air, crisp as a whispered tune,
Invites us to sway beneath the moon.
With every step, new stories told,
In frozen beauty, hearts unfold.

Footprints etch on the icy ground,
Echoes of magic, pure and profound.
Winter's breath, a fleeting sigh,
In the tapestry, we dare to fly.

A fleeting moment, soon it fades,
But in our soul, the memory stays.
The frosty tapestry will gleam,
A winter's dream, a lover's dream.

Timeless Elegance in the Cold

Wrapped in silence, the world waits,
As winter holds its breath and states.
The trees adorned, a crystal crown,
In this elegance, we won't drown.

Each flake whispers of grace untold,
A touch of magic in the cold.
The moonlight bathes the scene in glow,
Timeless beauty in purest snow.

Gentle winds weave a soft refrain,
Carrying scents of joy and pain.
In every heartbeat, echoes chime,
A winter's dance, a glimpse of time.

With every twirl, the stars express,
A story wrapped in stillness, blessed.
In this frozen land, we find our way,
Timeless elegance, here to stay.

As shadows stretch and daylight wanes,
We gather warmth from winter's chains.
In every corner, love unfolds,
In timeless elegance, spirits bold.

Veiled Radiance of the Woods

In shadows deep, where secrets lie,
The woods are veiled beneath the sky.
A canvas draped in silver light,
Whispers of magic, day and night.

Each pathway glimmers with fresh snow,
A secret world where few may go.
Beneath the boughs, the silence reigns,
Veiled radiance, a soft refrains.

Woven like dreams, the branches bend,
In nature's arms, our hearts commend.
Lost in wonder, we roam so free,
This winter's grip, a subtle plea.

Every rustle, a tale to tell,
From barren trees to icy well.
In crisp air, the joy unfolds,
Veiled radiance, as life beholds.

As twilight drapes its gentle cloak,
The woods awaken, and shadows spoke.
In nature's hush, we feel the grace,
Veiled radiance, our sacred space.

Nature's Winter Portrait

Brush strokes of white on a canvas bare,
Nature's portrait, a frosty affair.
Each flake drops like a whispered dream,
Framed in silence, a perfect theme.

The sun peeks through, a golden ray,
Kissing the snow in a gentle sway.
The trees, they shimmer, adorned in light,
Nature's art, a wondrous sight.

Footprints trace paths in the snow so deep,
Where stories linger, memories keep.
Each moment cherished, strong and bright,
A winter's canvas, kissed by light.

As dusk descends with a hush so clear,
The stars emerge, our dreams draw near.
In nature's embrace, we find our heart,
In winter's portrait, we play our part.

So let us wander, through this white maze,
In every moment, a spark of praise.
Nature's winter, forever we'll adore,
In its portrait, we will explore.

The Soft Touch of Frost

Morning whispers soft and light,
Frosty kisses greet the day.
Nature's blanket, pure and white,
Hides the world in quiet play.

Branches bow with heavy lace,
Sparkling jewels on every bough.
Winter's breath leaves a delicate trace,
In the stillness, wonders grow.

Footprints crunch on icy ground,
Echoes dance in frosty air.
Silence reigns, a soothing sound,
Magic lingers everywhere.

As the sun begins to rise,
Glistening flakes start to melt.
Nature winks with sparkling eyes,
In this charm, our hearts have dwelt.

A fleeting moment, pure delight,
In the softness, we will trust.
Hold it close, this frosty sight,
A treasure wrapped in frozen dust.

Dreaming Under Frosty Canopies

Stars above like diamonds shine,
Underneath the frosty trees.
Whispers of a world divine,
Carried softly on the breeze.

Dreamers gather, hearts aligned,
In the shade of icy limbs.
Silent stories intertwined,
Where the night's serenity swims.

Moonlight drapes its gentle glow,
Painting patterns on the ground.
In this hush, time seems to slow,
Magic in the air is found.

Winter's breath on our skin,
Chills the world but warms the soul.
Underneath this quilted grin,
We find peace that makes us whole.

In the quiet, dreams will soar,
On the wings of frost and night.
We awaken wanting more,
In the dark, we find our light.

Petals of Ice on Timber Tips

Morning glories wrapped in frost,
Petals glimmer, soft and bright.
Nature's wonders, never lost,
Timber tips aglow tonight.

In the stillness, beauty lies,
Every branch adorned with care.
Fragile gifts that captivate eyes,
Glistening under winter's stare.

As the wind begins to sing,
Chiming softly through the wood.
Life returns on winter's wing,
Creating beauty where it stood.

Whispers dance from tree to tree,
In the air of frozen dreams.
Nature's art, wild and free,
Where magic flows in silver streams.

Petals cling to branches tight,
As the world envelops night.
In these moments, pure delight,
Frozen wonders take their flight.

Embrace of the Chill

Winter wraps the earth in peace,
A gentle hush envelops all.
In this realm, our worries cease,
In frosty arms, we feel the call.

Chill of night ignites the stars,
Every twinkle, a distant song.
Quiet sighs and cold avatars,
A lullaby where we belong.

Underneath the blanket white,
Dreams arise like snowflakes fall.
In this wonder, pure delight,
Nature cradles every soul.

Fires crackle, warmth within,
Gathered close, we share our tales.
Finding joy where we begin,
A journey woven with the gales.

Moments freeze but hearts ignite,
In the chill, we find our fire.
Holding close this winter night,
As the frost fulfills desire.

Serenity among the Branches

Soft light filters through leaves,
Gentle breeze carries whispers,
Nature sings its quiet song,
Calmly, the world slows down.

Birds flutter in easy flight,
Nestled high among the boughs,
Moments of peace intertwine,
With the rustle of the trees.

A hidden brook lightly flows,
Sparkling under the sun's gaze,
Dappled shadows dance around,
In a tranquil embrace of green.

Every heartbeat syncs with nature,
As the day begins to fade,
A sense of timeless presence,
In this haven, all is well.

Clouds drift lazily above,
Casting shadows on the ground,
In this place of pure stillness,
Serenity breathes deeply here.

Twilight's Glint on Snowbound Pines

In the hush of twilight's glow,
Pines wear crowns of sparkling white,
Crystal flakes catch fading light,
A world wrapped in soft silence.

Stars emerge one by one,
Beneath the deepening blue,
The air is crisp, sharply clear,
Magic weaves through the trees.

Footsteps crunch on powdery snow,
Each sound a note of peace,
Whispers of winter's embrace,
Echoing through the still night.

Nature holds its breath in awe,
As shadows stretch and grow,
A moment frozen in time,
Where dreams dance among the pines.

Beneath the moon's gentle watch,
Night blankets the quiet earth,
In this place, wonder lingers,
Twilight's glint a precious gift.

Winter's Ethereal Mark

A tapestry of white unfolds,
Each flake a unique design,
Winter paints the world anew,
In strokes of soft, gentle grace.

Barren branches lace the sky,
Crowned with diamonds, they shine,
The air, crisp, fills the lungs,
A chill that awakens the heart.

Frozen ponds, mirroring dreams,
Reflecting stars in tranquil depths,
Nature's canvas stretches wide,
A silent brilliance all around.

Every path dressed in white lace,
Footprints tell of wanderers' tales,
Among the hush, life carries on,
Resilience wrapped in winter's hold.

As evening settles, shadows dance,
In the glow of a winter's night,
Ethereal beauty lingers on,
In every breath, every spark.

The Whispering Pines at Dusk

As dusk cloaks the fading light,
Whispering pines sigh softly low,
Their secrets swirling in the breeze,
Nature's lullaby unfolds.

Shadows stretch along the ground,
Drawing near the twilight's glow,
Gentle murmurs of the night,
Set the woods into a dream.

Breezes carry tales of old,
Each whisper wrapped in twilight,
Stories etched in ancient bark,
Guarded by the watchful trees.

Silhouettes rise against the sky,
Dark forms against the fading sun,
A world transformed, hushed yet alive,
In this moment, peace prevails.

The stars begin their twinkling dance,
Painting dreams on the canvas vast,
In the cradle of the pines,
The heartbeat of the earth lives on.

The Untold Stories of the Forest

In shadows deep, the secrets lie,
Beneath the boughs, where whispers sigh.
Old paths of moss, where few have tread,
In silent woods, the tales are spread.

Ancient trees hold memories tight,
Of creatures that danced in the pale moonlight.
A rustle, a footstep, a fleeting glance,
In the forest's heart, there's always a chance.

The owls hoot stories of ages past,
They watch the night like a spell that's cast.
With every breeze, a new tale is spun,
In the cool embrace of the setting sun.

Roots intertwined, like love's embrace,
Each ring a memory, in time and space.
Nature's canvas, painted so bright,
The forest sings softly, a sweet lullaby of night.

From tiny seedlings to giants tall,
Each voice echoes, reminding us all.
In the woods, where we often lose track,
The untold stories always bring us back.

Mystic Frosts and Whispering Pines

In the hush of night, frost blankets the ground,
Whispering pines share secrets profound.
Each crystal glimmers, a star in repose,
Beneath the moon's light, a spell that it chose.

Branches bow low, laden with dreams,
Captured moments in silvery gleams.
Echoes of laughter, bound in the chill,
Time dances lightly, serene and still.

The air is crisp, alive with the night,
Frosted whispers take delicate flight.
Beneath the surface, warm stories unfold,
Of friendships cherished and memories bold.

In each tiny flake, magic is found,
A canvas of wonder spreads all around.
While the world drifts into a tranquil sleep,
Mystic frost offers solace, its secrets to keep.

The pines hold their ground, steadfast and true,
With every season, they welcome the dew.
Woven in silence, their tales intertwine,
In the calm of the winter, the stars brightly shine.

Frosted Dreams in the Stillness

In the still of night, dreams take their flight,
Frosted landscapes bathed in soft light.
Each breath is visible, a cloud in the air,
Wrapped in the silence, a moment to share.

Crystalline blankets cover the trees,
Whispers of magic carried on the breeze.
As shadows lengthen, visions unfold,
In the chill of the night, tales begin to be told.

Stars twinkle gently, winking from high,
Painting a picture against the night sky.
The world, a canvas, so quiet and bright,
Frosted dreams dance in the stillness of night.

Frozen moments, like laughter long past,
Capture the essence, forever to last.
With a hush and a sigh, the night softly glows,
In the heart of the stillness, pure beauty flows.

As dawn approaches, the frost starts to fade,
But the dreams linger on, in a delicate shade.
In wonder, we rise, as the world comes alive,
Frosted dreams in stillness, forever survive.

Enigma of the Winter Grove

Amidst the trees, shadows softly creep,
In the winter grove, secrets run deep.
Each flake that falls brings a story untold,
Of echoing laughter and memories of old.

The air feels thick with a haunting refrain,
As whispers of winter call out in vain.
Branches entwined, a web of the past,
Guardians of time, with their stories amassed.

Beneath the frost, a pulse can be felt,
The language of nature, in silence is dealt.
Each rustling leaf, a mystery confined,
The enigma of growth, in the chill intertwined.

Where shadows linger and silence consumes,
The heartbeat of winter in every bloom.
Nature's enigma lies wrapped in the cold,
A tapestry woven, rich stories unfold.

As the sun rises, casting warmth on the glade,
The secrets awaken, no longer delayed.
In the light of the morning, the grove is alive,
The enigma revealed, where the wild things thrive.

A Canvas of Silver in Shadows

In twilight's embrace, shadows play,
Whispers of night float softly away.
Glimmers of silver, a painter's delight,
Each stroke a sigh in the hush of night.

Branches entwined in a dance of grace,
Moonbeams cascade, a tender trace.
In this twilight realm, dreams start to weave,
A canvas of silver, where hearts believe.

Stars look down, like eyes of the past,
Shimmering tales of the moments that last.
In the cool air, a lullaby flows,
Each note a secret the darkness knows.

Footsteps are silent, the night holds its breath,
Life and its stories entwined with death.
In the shadows, we find our way,
A canvas painted in shades of gray.

Yet in the dark, hope glimmers bright,
Guiding lost souls with a flickering light.
With each gentle step, we yearn and roam,
In shadows, we craft a dream-filled home.

Frosty Luminescence

Beneath the frost, the world glows white,
Crystals dance softly in the moon's light.
Trees wear a blanket, shimmering true,
In a winter's embrace, all feels brand new.

Stars twinkle bright in the frosty air,
Nature's quiet touch, a magic rare.
Each breath we take, clouds rise and float,
Whispers of winter wrapped 'round our coat.

Time seems to pause, the earth holds its sigh,
Under the frost, dreams begin to fly.
In the stillness, we find our peace,
As the cold winds sing, our worries cease.

A world made of silver, a soft retreat,
With each frosty step, our hearts skip a beat.
Embracing the chill, we feel alive,
In this frosty glow, our spirits thrive.

As dawn approaches, the sun will call,
Melting the frost, it touches us all.
Yet in the cold, memories remain,
Of frosty luminescence, sweet as rain.

The Crystalline Cathedral

In the heart of winter, a cathedral stands,
Crafted of crystals, shaped by nature's hands.
Sunlight cascades through its icy frame,
A prism of colors, each one a flame.

Whispers of silence fill the vast space,
Echoing dreams that time can't erase.
Every corner holds a story untold,
In this crystalline haven, both shy and bold.

Stalactites hang like chandeliers bright,
Reflecting the wonders of day and night.
In this frozen realm, peace can be found,
As the soft snow blankets the hallowed ground.

Step lightly through arches of glimmering grace,
In this sacred place, find solace and space.
Each crystal a promise, each beam a prayer,
In the cathedral's heart, we linger and stare.

As dusk descends, the world seems to fade,
Bathed in the glow of the ice serenade.
Here, in the stillness, our spirits entwine,
In the crystalline cathedral, we feel divine.

Dreaming in the Chill

In the hush of winter, we find our dreams,
Wrapped in the chill, beneath silver beams.
Snowflakes fall softly, crafting pure white,
In the silence we cherish, deep in the night.

With every heartbeat, the cold winds wail,
Telling of stories, of journeys we hail.
In the frosty air, hopes take flight,
Dreaming together, our souls ignite.

Each breath a crystal, a moment profound,
In this wintry wonder, our hearts resound.
Walking through shadows, we seek the light,
In the glow of the night, everything feels right.

Embracing the chill, we dance with the stars,
In the magic of winter, we heal our scars.
Lost in the moment, we drift and sway,
Dreaming in the chill, come what may.

As dawn arrives with a blush on the sky,
We wake from our dreams, no reason to cry.
For in the cold, our spirits will fill,
In the heart of winter, we still find our thrill.

Silent Brow of the Snowy Silent Pines

Silent sentinels stand tall,
Draped in white, they cradle all.
Softly whispers chill the air,
Nature's breath, beyond compare.

Beneath the boughs, shadows play,
In the silence, dreams sway.
Each flake falls with gentle grace,
Blanketing the earth's embrace.

The moonlight glistens on the ground,
In the quiet, peace is found.
Every branch holds secrets tight,
In the cloak of silver night.

Footsteps muffled, whispers low,
In this realm, time seems to slow.
Pines collect the falling snow,
While the night wraps all in flow.

Understars that softly glow,
Nature's heart beats very slow.
In this world of white and green,
Beauty lies, forever seen.

Whispers in the Gleaming White

Whispers dance on frosty air,
Tales of winter everywhere.
Softly falling, moonlit light,
Gleaming white, so pure, so bright.

Shadows stretch beneath the trees,
Carried gently by the breeze.
Snowflakes twirl in silent flight,
Cloaked in harmony of night.

Each breath forms a fleeting mist,
Moments that we can't resist.
Branches bow with snowy weight,
In this calm, we meditate.

Listen close to nature's sigh,
As the world breathes, wonders lie.
In the silence, hearts are free,
Nestled deep in winter's plea.

Beneath the stars, whispers grow,
Hints of life beneath the snow.
In the gleam of softest white,
Magic dwells, a pure delight.

Beneath the Frosted Canopy

Beneath the frost, a world concealed,\nIn the hush, our fate revealed.
Branches laden, soft and light,
Winter sings its tranquil rite.

Footprints fade in diamond dust,
Memory woven, silent trust.
Icicles hang, shimmering bright,
Nature's jewels in blinding light.

Every whisper holds a tale,
In the stillness, dreams prevail.
Soft shadows weave a tapestry,
Of magic lost in reverie.

Amidst the pines, the heart finds peace,
In this moment, all else cease.
Beneath each flake so deftly spun,
Harmony beneath the sun.

Take a breath, embrace the cold,
In the silence, life unfolds.
Underneath this frosted dome,
Winter whispers us back home.

The Whispering Silence of Winter Pines

The winter pines stand tall and wise,
Underneath the quiet skies.
Whispers float on gentle winds,
Nature's lullaby begins.

Snowflakes kiss the forest floor,
Silent promises to restore.
In the hush, the heartbeats blend,
As nature speaks, our souls transcend.

Branches sway with secrets old,
Stories in the silence told.
Frozen moments, still and bright,
Captured in the silver light.

Every sigh a spark of grace,
In the stillness, we find our place.
Among the pines, the world is good,
Here, we feel all understood.

In this church of nature's calm,
Winter offers soothing balm.
The whispering silence intertwines,
With our spirit, where the pines.

Resplendent Silence in the Pines

In the stillness, whispers weave,
Tall pines stand like ancient guards.
Sunlight dapples the forest floor,
Each shadow a memory restored.

Branches sway with the softest breeze,
Nature's breath, a gentle hymn.
Underneath, life quietly thrives,
In the silence, peace begins.

Footsteps hush on the carpeted ground,
Mossy layers cradle the sound.
A world untold beneath the boughs,
In solitude, the heart bows.

Every sound, a sacred song,
Echoes dance where dreams belong.
Resplendent calm fills the air,
Life unfolds without a care.

In the pines, tranquility reigns,
Each moment, a treasure gained.
Silence whispers through the trees,
In their embrace, the spirit frees.

The Magic of a Frost-Flecked Twilight

Twilight drapes in silver light,
Frosty whispers paint the night.
Gentle hues of pale blue glow,
A magic moment, soft and slow.

Shadows grow as the sun dips low,
Magic dances in the snow.
Silvery crystals glitter bright,
Silent wonders fill the sight.

Each breath mist, a fleeting sigh,
Horizon kisses the starry sky.
Hope is woven with every gleam,
In this twilight, all is dream.

Nature rests, cocooned in peace,
As the chill sets in, all worries cease.
Wrapped in magic, hearts take flight,
In the beauty of the frost-kissed night.

With every step, a crunching sound,
The whispers of the season surround.
In this moment, souls entwine,
Lost in the magic, we align.

Crystal Dreams Beneath Evergreen

Beneath the green, dreams softly lie,
In crystal visions, spirits fly.
Whispering winds through branches sway,
Where memories dance and shadows play.

Gentle glimmers of morning dew,
Awakening hearts with every view.
In the hush of the dawn's embrace,
Nature's grace leaves a warm trace.

The air is thick with lingering light,
As visions swirl in emerald night.
Every breath a tale untold,
In the woodland, life unfolds.

Little creatures weave and roam,
In the stillness, they find home.
Crystal dreams in every leaf,
Nature whispers sweet relief.

Awake, alive in colors bright,
Beneath evergreen, pure delight.
In this sanctuary, souls revive,
Amidst the dreams, we feel alive.

The Charmed Silence of Winter Woods

In winter woods, a hush prevails,
Blankets white on winding trails.
Silence wraps the world in grace,
Each flake, a soft, enchanting lace.

Crystal branches, lifeless yet bold,
Guard secrets of stories untold.
Footprints etch upon the snow,
Where moments linger, softly glow.

A breath of frost in the chilled air,
Nature rests with tender care.
In the quiet, echoes sing,
Charmed by what the stillness brings.

Whispers of trees in frozen sleep,
While the heart of winter keeps.
Each sigh a note in nature's song,
In this silence, we all belong.

Time stands still near frosty pines,
In the woods, a peace divine.
As twilight falls, shadows blend,
In charmed silence, we transcend.

The Stillness Between the Pines

In the forest where silence sighs,
Whispers dance beneath the skies.
Tall pines stand like sentinels,
Guarding tales the soft breeze tells.

Moss carpets the ground in green,
Nature's hush, a soothing scene.
Sunlight filters, a golden stream,
Awakening dreams from slumber's theme.

Each needle sways with gentle grace,
Time slows down in this sacred place.
A moment held in nature's palm,
Where peace wraps all in its calming balm.

The air is fresh, a crisp delight,
Embracing all who seek the light.
Underneath the boughs so tall,
Nature's peace enfolds us all.

As shadows stretch and evening falls,
A nightingale sweetly calls.
In the stillness, hearts align,
Finding solace, pure, divine.

Shimmering Shadows in the Cold

Underneath the frozen moon,
Whispers weave a crystal tune.
Shadows shimmer, soft and pale,
Enchanting all within the vale.

Icicles hang from branches bare,
A spark of magic fills the air.
Frosty breath of winter's grace,
Turns the world into a lace.

Each twinkle on the snowlit ground,
A dance of light, a silent sound.
As stars peek through the velvet night,
Nature dons her cloak of white.

The chill wraps close, a tender hug,
In winter's realm, the world is snug.
Footsteps crunch on the frozen floor,
Echoes of adventures galore.

As dawn approaches, colors rise,
Painting warmth across the skies.
In shimmering shadows, young and old,
Find stories waiting to be told.

Nature's Cloak of Tranquility

In the meadow, calm flows wide,
Nature's beauty, a gentle guide.
Softly rustles the emerald grass,
Time meanders, moments pass.

Birds serenade the breaking dawn,
Each note a promise, a new fawn.
Butterflies glimmer in the sun,
Whispers of life, all is one.

Underneath the flowering boughs,
Every leaf a sacred vow.
The breeze carries secrets untold,
Wrapped in beauty, hearts unfold.

No rush to chase the fleeting hour,
In stillness lies true power.
Nature teaches with every sigh,
To pause, reflect, and simply try.

As twilight drapes its velvet hue,
Stars appear, a dazzling view.
In nature's arms, we find our way,
A tranquil heart, our souls at play.

The Nymphs of Winter's Grove

In the glade where silence breathes,
Nymphs weave magic 'neath the leaves.
Snowflakes swirl in frosty dance,
Enticing dreams to take a chance.

With every step on crunchy snow,
Ancient tales of winter flow.
Gentle laughter fills the air,
In their presence, free from care.

Twilight whispers secrets low,
In the grove, the soft lights glow.
Nymphs of winter, fair and bright,
Guide the lost into the night.

With every breeze, a soft embrace,
Nature cradles time and space.
In this realm where spirits play,
Joy blossoms in shades of gray.

As the moonlight paints the ground,
Magic stirs in every sound.
The nymphs of winter, wise and bold,
Share their warmth against the cold.

Frost-Kissed Whisper

The morning frost does gently cling,
A silver veil on everything.
Soft whispers dance upon the air,
As winter's breath is everywhere.

The trees stand still, their branches bare,
In quietude, a world so rare.
A fleeting touch of icy grace,
Each crystal spark a warm embrace.

The sun awakes, a timid glow,
Beneath the chill, the heartbeats flow.
Nature's hymn begins to rise,
Beneath the brightening skies.

In harmony, the shadows play,
As dawn unfolds a brighter day.
Each moment pure, a treasured find,
In frosty whispers, dreams unwind.

With every breath, the silence grows,
A peaceful pause where beauty shows.
Through winter's veil, the spirit sings,
In frost-kissed whispers, love takes wing.

Moonlight Among Boughs

The moonlight spills through leafy grace,
Illuminating night's embrace.
Beneath the stars, the shadows weave,
A place where dreams might dare believe.

Soft glimmers dance like whispered sighs,
As gentle breezes stir the skies.
Among the branches, secrets hide,
In every rustle, whispers glide.

The nightingale calls, a sweet refrain,
Echoing softly through the lane.
In moonlit gardens, hearts entwine,
As nature paints with strokes divine.

Dappled light on petals bright,
Transforms the world into pure delight.
With each step taken, magic flows,
In moonlight's grasp, true beauty glows.

So let us wander, hand in hand,
Through silver woods, a dreamland grand.
With hearts aglow, we'll find our way,
In moonlight's soft and tender sway.

The Chill Beneath the Canopy

In shadowed woods where echoes dwell,
The chill unfolds its icy shell.
Beneath the canopy of leaves,
A subtle hush, the forest breathes.

The branches sway with whispered tones,
As twilight deepens, night atones.
Cool breezes carry tales untold,
Of nature's grace and secrets bold.

Each step reveals a world of peace,
From worries past, a sweet release.
In twilight's hush, the heart can soar,
As shadows beckon to explore.

The chill might bite, but warmth resides,
In every nook where spirit hides.
Embrace the night, the stars will guide,
As whispers of the earth abide.

In woven dreams, the chill transforms,
The chill beneath in quiet warms.
Among the trees, where silence reaps,
A tranquil heart in slumber sleeps.

Glimmers in the Gloom

Through dusky paths where shadows creep,
A flicker glows, the secrets keep.
In every corner, hope prevails,
As magic weaves its tender trails.

Beneath the weight of heavy night,
The stars emerge, a guiding light.
With every breath, the darkness fades,
In glimmers bright, the charm cascades.

The cool air whispers, soft and low,
While hidden wonders start to show.
A melody of dreams set free,
In every heart, a quiet plea.

Though gloom may linger, fears shall fade,
For light will pierce the shadows made.
Embrace the glow, the quiet hum,
In glimmers sweet, the dawn will come.

So let us walk where shadows blend,
In gentle night's embrace, we'll mend.
For in the dark, the light resumes,
With every heartbeat, glimmers bloom.

Enchanted by the Flurry

Snowflakes dance in twilight's glow,
Whispers of magic in the flow.
Winter's breath, a soft embrace,
Nature dons her crystal lace.

A world transformed, so pure and bright,
Under stars that twinkle at night.
Each flake falls with a gentle grace,
Creating peace in this sacred space.

Footsteps muffled, secrets kept,
Where dreams gather, and wonder leapt.
Heartbeats echo in the chill,
In the silence, time stands still.

Branches bow, adorned in white,
A tranquil symphony of light.
Magic lingers in the air,
As if enchantment waits somewhere.

Joyful laughter fills the breeze,
As snowmen rise beneath the trees.
Memories held in frosty sighs,
Underneath the winter skies.

Tranquil Stillness of the Woods

In the heart of the silent green,
Whispers linger, softly seen.
Leaves converse with gentle sighs,
A secret world beneath the skies.

Sunlight dapples on the ground,
Nature's melody, a soothing sound.
Each step taken, slow and kind,
A refuge found, a peace defined.

The brook hums low, a constant friend,
Through twisted paths that seem to bend.
Mossy carpets cradle the feet,
Where earth and spirit gently meet.

Shadows play between the trees,
Carried softly by the breeze.
In this realm of quiet art,
The woods embrace the weary heart.

Birds take flight, a soft refrain,
As sunlight breaks through after rain.
In every pause, in every glance,
Life unfolds in a gentle dance.

A sacred place where time is still,
Awakens hope and nurtures will.
In tranquil stillness, love resides,
In the calm where nature guides.

Frost-Kissed Conversations

On frosty mornings, world awakes,
Voices spark in the cozy lakes.
Chill in the air, warm hearts reside,
As nature's pulse beats soft, and wide.

Whispers dance on the frozen streams,
Echoes of gentle, fading dreams.
Every breath a cloud in the light,
Frost-kissed conversations take flight.

Over hills, the laughter rolls,
Uniting hearts, and warming souls.
Old stories shared beside the fire,
A tapestry woven, never tires.

In the stillness, hope takes root,
Life's sweet flavor, winter's fruit.
Each pause punctuated with grace,
Conversations in this sacred space.

Chasing shadows, seeking the sun,
Connecting hearts, the dance begun.
Frosted breath, like whispered vows,
In the cold, time gently bows.

All around, nature joins the spree,
A symphony of you and me.
In the cold, we find our spark,
Frost-kissed love ignites the dark.

Hushed Murmurs Among the Trees

In the grove where shadows dwell,
Softly nature weaves her spell.
Murmurs rise with the evening breeze,
Secrets carried through the trees.

Petals drift in the twilight's grace,
While stars emerge in their rightful place.
A symphony played on leaves so high,
Hushed whispers float beneath the sky.

Crickets chirp their nightly tune,
As the world wears a somber rune.
Each blade of grass, a silent muse,
In this sanctuary, the heart peruse.

A tender hush, the world asleep,
In shadows deep, the secrets keep.
Time meanders, slow and free,
In the murmurs among the trees.

Branches sway, the moonlight glows,
Illuminating the path that flows.
Soft caresses of the night,
In the quiet, we find our light.

And as the dawn begins to break,
With every breath, our spirits wake.
In each moment, life's sweet tease,
Found in hushed murmurs, among the trees.

Woven Dreams of the Cold Night

Under stars, whispers float,
Silent wishes, dreams remote.
Moonlight drapes in silver hue,
A tapestry of night so true.

Frosty air, a breath of calm,
In the darkness, a soothing balm.
Shadows dance on snowflake trails,
While the heart of winter wails.

Woven paths of shimmering light,
Guide the lost through the cold night.
In this world of crisp delight,
Hope ignites, burning bright.

Echoes swirl in frozen glee,
Murmurs of old, wild and free.
Beneath the weight of icy dreams,
Life awakens, or so it seems.

Embrace the chill, let spirits soar,
In woven dreams, forevermore.
From the depths of winter's grasp,
We find warmth within, we clasp.

The Frost's Gentle Caress

Morning breaks with a tender touch,
Frosty hands that feel so much.
Nature whispers soft and low,
In the glimmering, pristine glow.

Each blade of grass, a jeweled prize,
Underneath the pale blue skies.
Trees adorned in crystal lace,
A quiet, sweet, enchanting space.

With every breath, a cloud of white,
A fleeting moment, pure delight.
The world transformed by winter's art,
A masterpiece, a frozen heart.

As sunlight warms the chilly air,
Frost's gentle kiss, a loving care.
Though icy nights may come and go,
Morning brings a warming glow.

Embrace the frost, let it remain,
In its beauty, there's no pain.
For every chill, a spark of cheer,
The frost's caress keeps love near.

Clarity in the Winter Stillness

Snowflakes fall with whispered grace,
Each is unique in its soft space.
Silvery silence, soft embrace,
Winter's breath—nature's pace.

Crystal air clears the mind,
In stillness, peace is what we find.
A moment captured, time stands still,
Echoes lost on the frosty hill.

Beneath the white, life waits and dreams,
In the quiet, a spirit beams.
Branches like lace against the sky,
Painting beauty as hours fly.

Clarity in the quiet hour,
Every flake holds hidden power.
With every breath, a spark ignites,
In winter's heart, hope takes flights.

Embrace the calm, the world at rest,
In winter's beauty, we are blessed.
Every moment, pure and bright,
Brings clarity in the quiet night.

Frostborne Blessings from the Forest

The forest sleeps in icy dreams,
Frost adorns the silent streams.
A blanket white, it softly lays,
On the earth, where stillness plays.

In the boughs, a gentle sigh,
Leaves whisper as they pass by.
Nature's hush, a secret shared,
In the cold, we are ensnared.

Every step on softened ground,
A muffled world, lost and found.
The breath of winter fills the air,
Frostborne blessings everywhere.

Sunrise paints the frosted trees,
Glittering under the soft breeze.
Whispers of life in every breath,
In the forest, love conquers death.

Wander deep through winter's grace,
In the stillness, find your place.
With each moment, feel the glow,
Frostborne blessings that we know.

Secrets Beneath the Powder

In the still of winter's breath,
Lies a world draped in white,
Whispers hidden in the snow,
Secrets waiting for the light.

Beneath the powder's soft embrace,
Footprints tell of journeys past,
Echoes hidden in the lace,
Memories fading, fading fast.

A quiet realm of silence deep,
Where shadows dance and secrets dwell,
Nature's hearth, a spell to keep,
In the thrall of winter's spell.

Unravel whispers, soft and low,
Feel the pulse of buried dreams,
The hidden tales that yearn to flow,
In the light of tender beams.

Every flake a story cast,
In the tapestry of frost,
Underneath the chill, steadfast,
Secrets here are never lost.

Shadows of the Silent Grove

In the heart of a silent grove,
Where the ancient secrets sigh,
Shadows whisper tales of love,
In the dappled light gone by.

Trees stand tall, their branches sway,
Guardians of the quiet night,
In their arms, the lost decay,
Underneath the moon's pale light.

Footsteps soft on mossy ground,
Nature cradles every sound,
In the stillness, dreams abound,
With the echoes all around.

Leaves rustle like secrets shared,
In a dance of dusk and dawn,
Ancient hearts gently bared,
In the twilight, all are drawn.

Breathe the magic, feel it swell,
In the shadows woven tight,
A hidden story, weaves a spell,
In the silence of the night.

Crystal Veils of Twilight

When twilight falls and shadows blend,
A canvas painted in soft hues,
Crystal veils that secrets send,
In the dusk, the world renews.

Stars awaken one by one,
Sprinkling light on earth so dear,
The day bows low, its battles won,
As the night begins to steer.

Whispers float on gentle breeze,
Carrying tales of yesteryear,
In the branches, rustling leaves,
Cloaked in twilight's tender sphere.

Glimmers twinkling, dreams take flight,
In the hush of evening's grace,
Every moment feels so right,
Time slows down, a warm embrace.

Hold your breath, for here we stand,
In the crystal twilight's balm,
With every heartbeat, take your hand,
In the magic, find your calm.

The Whispering Woods in White

Through the whispering woods so white,
Blanketed in a silent hush,
Every branch a flickering light,
In the winter's gentle crush.

Snowflakes dance like memories,
Swirling softly from above,
In the stillness, time agrees,
Nature's way of showing love.

Footsteps imprint stories deep,
Winding paths through timeless trees,
In the hollows, secrets sleep,
Carried on the winter breeze.

Feel the magic, taste the air,
With each breath, a world unfolds,
In this realm, without a care,
Whispers shared, and tales retold.

Embrace the chill, the night ignites,
In the woods where shadows weave,
Every heartbeat, pure delights,
In the white where dreams believe.

Lullaby of the Frosted Branches

Whispers of the icy breeze,
Gently sway the frosted trees.
Moonlight dances, soft and pale,
Nature sings a cozy tale.

Stars peek through the velvet night,
Blanketing the world so white.
Each branch draped in crystal lace,
Holds the stillness of this place.

A lullaby that softly lures,
Winter's magic gently pours.
Slumber's kiss on sleepy land,
Frosted branches, softly stand.

Dreamers nestle, hearts awaken,
In the hush, no sound is taken.
Frozen wonders come alive,
In the quiet, spirits thrive.

As dawn breaks, the chill will fade,
Yet the beauty will not jade.
Embers of this night will last,
In memories of winter's past.

Serenity in the Winter Lair

Nestled in the snow's embrace,
Time slows down in this still space.
Cotton clouds above the vale,
Whisper secrets, soft and frail.

The fireplace crackles, warmth surrounds,
In quiet joy, peace abounds.
Outside, harbingers of white,
Inside, we bask in cozy light.

Silence reigns with gentle touch,
Giving hearts a chance to clutch.
Each breath kissed by frosty air,
In this haven, none compare.

Snowflakes drift like whispered dreams,
Framing night in silver seams.
Stars come out to keep their watch,
While we slow our hurried watch.

As evening leaves its tender mark,
In winter's lair, we find our spark.
Serenity, a gift from snow,
In this silence, love will grow.

When the Forest Wears White

In a world that's dressed in white,
Everything feels pure and bright.
Trees adorned in crystal crowns,
Nature wears her fleeting gowns.

Echoes of the silence hum,
Footsteps light, the softest drum.
Animals seek warmth inside,
As winter's chill begins to bide.

Winds kiss every sleeping bough,
Time stands still, we wonder how.
Footprints trace where few have trod,
In stillness, we feel the prod.

Branches bow to hold the weight,
Of every flake that seals their fate.
Each gust brings a whispered sigh,
Underneath the vast, gray sky.

When the forest wears its white,
Every moment feels so right.
In this season, hearts align,
With nature's grace, our souls entwine.

Glowing Hearts in the Cold

Beneath the frost, our spirits gleam,
In winter's chill, we find our dream.
Hands clasped tight, we face the night,
Glowing hearts, a warm delight.

Snowflakes fall like whispered thoughts,
Nature's canvas, frost adorns.
With every laugh, the cold retreats,
In joyous sounds, our love repeats.

Candles flicker, shadows dance,
In gentle light, we find romance.
Starlit skies, a cosmic show,
Guiding us where warm winds blow.

Through frosted windows, joy is clear,
In every glance, we hold sincere.
Together, wrapped in winter's shawl,
In glowing hearts, we have it all.

As seasons change, and time will flow,
Let memories of warmth still grow.
In the cold of night, hope imbues,
Our glowing hearts, our winter muse.

Milton Keynes UK
Ingram Content Group UK Ltd.
UKHW010231111224
452348UK00011B/674